CW01192722

Celebrating the endless curiosity of Johnny Barcroft, with love - CB

For Jon and Liz, with love - SW

For Mum, with love and thanks for all of the envelopes! - AH

Brimming with creative inspiration, how-to projects, and useful information to enrich your everyday life, Quarto Knows is a favourite destination for those pursuing their interests and passions. Visit our site and dig deeper with our books into your area of interest: Quarto Creates, Quarto Cooks, Quarto Homes, Quarto Lives, Quarto Drives, Quarto Explores, Quarto Gifts, or Quarto Kids.

The publishers and authors would like to thank David Boyle for his invaluable advice and support as consultant for this book.

Text © 2020 Catherine Barr and Steve Williams.
Illustrations © 2020 Amy Husband.

First published in 2020 by Frances Lincoln Children's Books, an imprint of The Quarto Group.
The Old Brewery, 6 Blundell Street, London N7 9BH, United Kingdom.
T (0)20 7700 6700 F (0)20 7700 8066 www.QuartoKnows.com

The right of Catherine Barr and Steve Williams to be identified as the authors and Amy Husband to be identified as the illustrator of this work has been asserted by them in accordance with the Copyright, Designs and Patents Act, 1988 (United Kingdom).

All rights reserved.
No part of this publication may be reproduced, stored in a retrieval system, or transmitted, in any form, or by any means, electrical, mechanical, photocopying, recording or otherwise without the prior written permission of the publisher or a licence permitting restricted copying.
A catalogue record for this book is available from the British Library.

ISBN 978-0-7112-4536-5

The illustrations were created with mixed media and collage
Set in Gill Sans

Published by Katie Cotton and Georgia Amson-Bradshaw
Designed by Sasha Moxon
Edited by Claire Grace
Production by Nicolas Zeifman

Manufactured in Guangdong, China TT022020

9 8 7 6 5 4 3 2 1

MIX
Paper from responsible sources
FSC® C008047

The Story of
INVENTIONS

A first book about world-changing discoveries

Catherine Barr and **Steve Williams**
Illustrated by **Amy Husband**

Frances Lincoln
Children's Books

Wheels were first invented in the Bronze Age and they changed the world. Potters used flat wheels to spin their pots in busy cities.

It took time to harness horses and invent tools to make wheels spin on carts. But when they did, these carts became chariots that gathered speed with spokes. They bumped across Asia to Egypt, where they carried Egyptian archers into war. These wobbly wheels changed the story of war forever.

Mind my ears!

Biofuel

3500 BCE Invention of wheel

Romans built smooth roads for their chariots and added bounce with something called suspension. In time, people worked out how to make tyres from rubber and today all kinds of wheels roll around Earth and rove off-road on Mars.

"Follow the North Star!"

On journeys long ago, people used the starry sky to map their way but got lost on cloudy days. Until a strange rock helped point the way.

Lodestone

Dangled on a thread, lodestone is a natural magnet that swings North. This early compass helped Chinese armies find enemies in the fog. In Europe, magnetic compasses helped sailors find their way in all weathers.

270 BCE Invention of compass

Over time, iron needles replaced lodestone and different compasses were designed for air, land and sea. Today satellites in space show us exactly where we are with an invention called GPS.

What a sticky mess.

In China, an emperor's official sat under a mulberry tree. He broke and mashed up some bark, mixed it with rags and water, pressed it and laid it flat. It dried into paper, which he used to wrap up precious things.

People began to scribble on it too – it was cheaper than using silk and lighter than bamboo. Chinese papermakers were captured to reveal their secrets, but far away people still scribbled on animal skins.

105 AD Invention of paper

"This is exciting news."

Later in Europe, a new printing press helped people make mountains of books with paper pages for everyone to read. Learning spread across the world. People wrote stories, poems and news that inspired ideas in changing times.

"I love The Story of Life!"

Is it time for tea?

Poor weather made keeping time difficult. Sundials that used the sun's shadow to tell the time failed on cloudy days. Streams of sand, burning candles and flowing water were all used to measure time by people long ago.

A Chinese monk made the first accurate time keeper with a water clock. Water triggered an hourly bell allowing people to keep track of time. Medieval monks made new clocks to time their prayers. Later clocks swung with heavy pendulums but time stopped ticking when no-one remembered to wind the clock up. Today most of us wear watches on our wrists. Problems? What problems?

Water clock

725 AD Invention of clocks

Pendulum clock

Wrist watch

A mineral called quartz solved the problem. Electricity from batteries make quartz vibrate with a regular rhythm, which helps keep the time. Now in space, atomic clocks tell the most accurate time of all – losing only a second every 15 billion years.

And you've lived THAT long to prove it.!?

Watches told time on the move

As time passed, populations grew.
Soldiers drew swords to defend their cities and land. They fought by hand, until an explosion in the East changed the weapons of war forever.

Bang, bang!

850 AD Invention of gunpowder

In China, experiments for a potion for eternal life went up in smoke. Gunpowder had been invented by mistake. The recipe for this mysterious black powder, which explodes when lit, passed from Asia along the Silk Road to Europe and beyond.

Gunpowder fuelled early cannons and guns and it led to the creation of modern armies. Now gunpowder also crackles in fireworks across our dark skies.

Coal fires sparked a revolution that powered a **much** faster pace of life.

Before coal was burned to make steam, machines, transport and tools were driven slowly by water, wind and horse power.

Toot, toot!

1712 Invention of steam engine

Pressure from the steam moved pistons, which powered engines. The first steam machines pumped water out of flooded English mines. They made it safer for miners to work deep underground. Soon people boarded puffing trains heading for new steam-powered factories. These noisy giants wove silk and cotton which were bundled into ships and traded around the world.

Oooh, smelly smoke!

Today coal and oil still power most electricity on Earth. But these fossil fuels are polluting our skies so sun, water and wind are once again being used to help us survive this threatening climate change.

Solar panels

During a time called the Industrial Revolution, disease spread in crowded cities. Smallpox spread most easily of all. Mysteriously, milkmaids were safe from this 'speckled monster' if they had caught a milder disease called cowpox.

1798 Invention of vaccinations

This gave an English doctor an idea. He gave a boy cowpox on purpose,
then exposed him to smallpox. The boy stayed well. The doctor realised
that catching cowpox had prepared the boy's body to fight smallpox.
From this experiment, the doctor invented the first vaccine.
In time, no-one in the world caught smallpox any more.

Vaccination now saves millions of lives. Each year there are new vaccines,
but scientists still battle to invent them for some deadly diseases.

"Clunk, clunk, clunk!"

Using a machine to do maths was an interesting new idea but no-one thought it could really work. However, people began to get excited about what might be possible.

1830s Invention of computers

In our modern world, computers make complicated information useful by helping us measure, explore and understand the world and ourselves. Computers map the Earth, control traffic, warn us about the weather and predict danger.

This is so fast, it's amazing!

The first computer cracked secret codes that helped win the second World War. Since then, more powerful computers have improved and changed people's lives. Some people wonder if these amazing machines might one day be cleverer than humans.

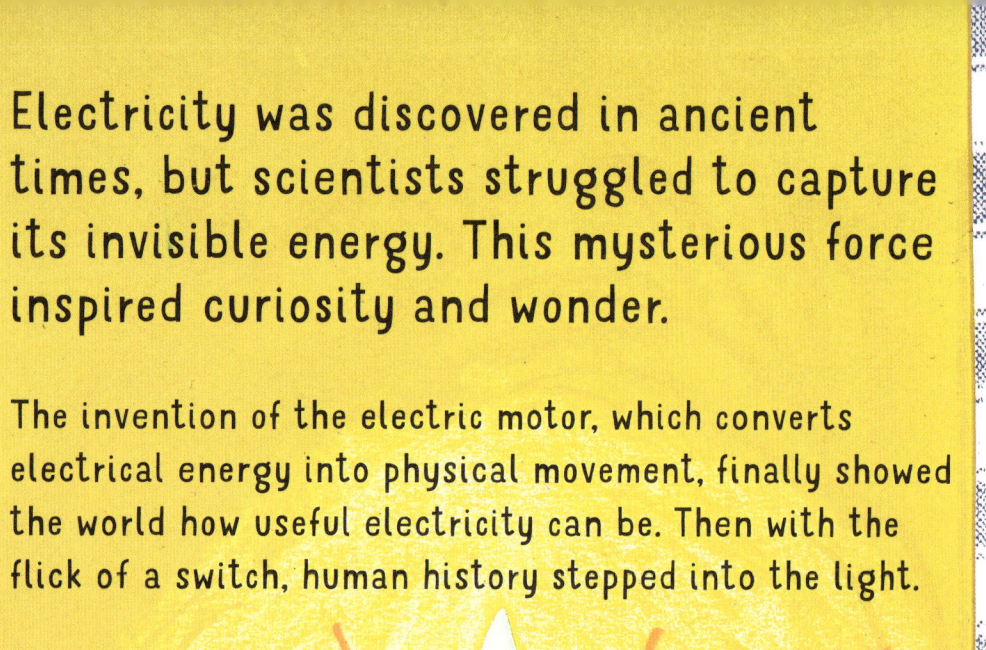

Electricity was discovered in ancient times, but scientists struggled to capture its invisible energy. This mysterious force inspired curiosity and wonder.

The invention of the electric motor, which converts electrical energy into physical movement, finally showed the world how useful electricity can be. Then with the flick of a switch, human history stepped into the light.

1832 Invention of electric motor

"Fancy a bedtime story?"

"Hopefully, I'll get a lie-in"

The electric bulb lit gloomy homes and life changed with the introduction of night work in factories that now had limitless light. Today our planet glitters in space. However, in remote places more than a billion people are still waiting to be able to turn on the light.

Electricity powers light, but it can also send messages.
This discovery sparked the invention of the telephone. Voices were turned into electric signals that travelled along copper wires, so people could speak to each other.

Giant cables were sailed out across the Atlantic to be laid on ocean floors linking Europe and America. Telephones rang and across the world people picked up to swap stories, information and gossip.
A telephone network began to spread.

Where?

What?

1876 Invention of telephones

The first smartphone was big and heavy. Now slim phones slide into pockets and decorate wrists. Today mobile phones connect the richest and the poorest people to the rest of the world.

Chatting by phone was instant but meeting up still took time.
Long journeys by horse or steam engines were dirty, noisy and smelly.

A new kind of engine made cars possible. The first cars were built one expensive part at a time. When they finally rolled out of factories, families piled in and traffic all over the world began to jam.

1886 Invention of cars

Horse poo made roads messy but cars spewed invisible, poisonous fumes. Electric cars and some with cleaner fuels are now zooming onto the roads but the climate is already changing fast. Campaigns to save our lungs and planet grow stronger as global temperatures rise.

Driverless car

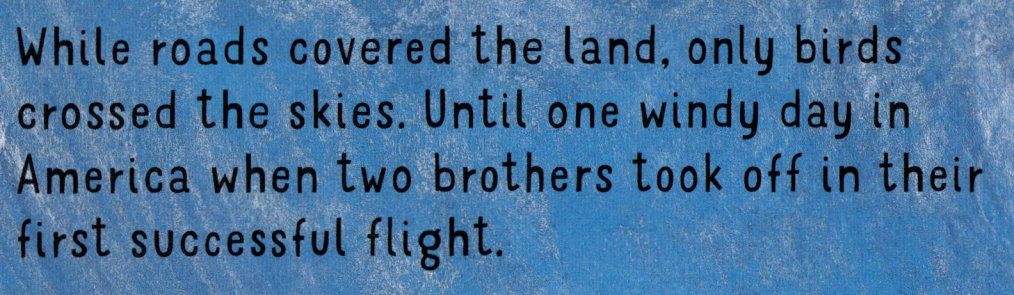

While roads covered the land, only birds crossed the skies. Until one windy day in America when two brothers took off in their first successful flight.

For 20 years, aeroplanes were packed with parcels and letters. Finally passengers climbed aboard and jumbo jets made flying cheap enough for holidays with a bird's eye view. But now air travel is cheap, lots of people fly. This is polluting our skies and costing the Earth.

1903 Invention of planes

"Next time can we get the train?"

"Watch out!"

People longed to go further, to the universe beyond. So humans invented a rocket and shot up into space. Space is now spinning with satellites and bits of junk that need tidying up.

Today, spacecraft look for new planets, while astronauts dream of life on Mars.

"What a mess."

Today life on Earth battles with plastic.
Plastic seemed fantastic because it can be tough, bendy, waterproof, thick, thin, colourful, colourless and cheap. It quickly became one of the most useful materials people had ever seen.

1907 Invention of plastic

"Hope that's a paper straw!"

Refillable bottle

Some plastic breaks down but it doesn't go away. So it is piling up, polluting and poisoning the planet. It trickles down our drains, clogs our rivers and swirls deep in our seas, harming underwater life.

This plastic tide is hard to stop. But by refusing single use plastic and recycling, we can help wildlife and protect the environment too.

Far from the ocean, World Wars raged on land. While soldiers fought, scientists in quiet, distant places puzzled the atom and its mysterious energy locked inside. Their work led to a monster invention – the biggest bomb the world had ever seen.

1945 Invention of nuclear weapons

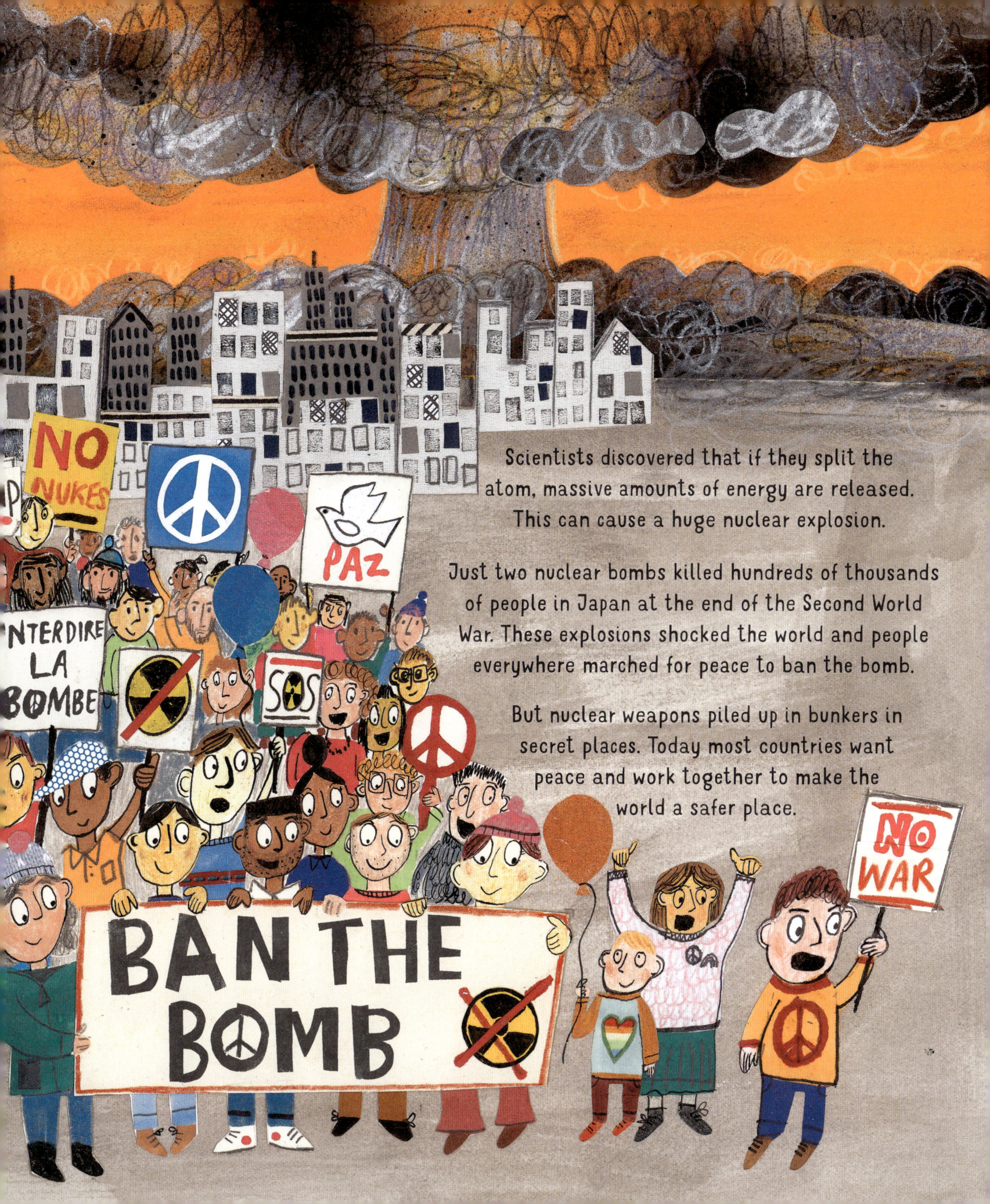

Scientists discovered that if they split the atom, massive amounts of energy are released. This can cause a huge nuclear explosion.

Just two nuclear bombs killed hundreds of thousands of people in Japan at the end of the Second World War. These explosions shocked the world and people everywhere marched for peace to ban the bomb.

But nuclear weapons piled up in bunkers in secret places. Today most countries want peace and work together to make the world a safer place.

Computers give us facts to make decisions about the way we live. With the invention of the internet, they have changed the kind of knowledge we share and the way we talk and listen.

Today Invention of internet

Computers can already do amazing things. They can predict how we feel and behave. They can play music to make us feel better. The smallest computer on Earth can measure the temperature of a cell and fits on a grain of rice.

In the future, computers will be smaller and cleverer than we can imagine. But how will humans use these inventions to care for each other and planet Earth? One day you may decide.

3500 BCE Invention of wheel   270 BCE Invention of compass

Today Invention of internet
1945 Invention of nuclear weapons
1907 Invention of plastic

Glossary of useful words

Atoms – tiny parts that everything in the universe is made from.

Biofuel – a type of fuel made from living matter.

Bronze Age – a period of time 4–6 thousand years ago, when bronze (a mixture of metals tin and copper) replaced stone for making things.

Cables – bundles of wires with protective casing that safely transport electricity.

Cells – tiny living things that are the building blocks of all life on Earth.

Civilisations – an organised way of people living peacefully together.

Climate change – long term changes in the world's climate. Today it is mostly caused by people burning oil, coal and gas as well as large scale deforestation (the cutting down of trees).

GPS – a way of working out where you are using satellites in space.

Internet – a global computer network.

Magnet – an object that has a magnetic field, which attracts other magnets and some metals.

Medieval – a period of time in history from around 600 AD to 1500 AD.

Mineral – a substance from the earth, usually in the rocks.

Monk – a religious person who spends his life following certain beliefs, with a simple life of prayer and work.

1903 Invention of planes   1886 Invention of cars

105 AD Invention of paper

725 AD Invention of clocks

850 AD Invention of gunpowder

1712 Invention of steam engine

1798 Invention of vaccinations

Pendulum – a hanging weight that swings from side to side helping clocks keep regular time.

Pistons – a part of an engine that slides up and down to make a machine work.

Potion – a drink that is supposed to contain poison or medicine that has a magical or special effect on someone.

Printing press – a machine used to print books, magazines and papers.

Recycling – changing materials that have been thrown away into something useful.

Revolution – a big sudden change affecting lots of people's lives.

Satellites – a small object in space that revolves around a bigger object.

Silk Road – a network of trade roads between Asia and Europe, used about 2,000 years ago.

Single-use plastic – plastic that is only used once then thrown away or recycled.

Smartphone – a mobile phone with lots of functions like a computer, with a touch screen and internet access.

Spokes – bars from the centre to the outside of a wheel, which make it stronger.

Sundials – an object used by people to tell the time using the shadow of the sun.

Suspension – in vehicles, this is a way of making travel less bumpy by adding springs to absorb the shock of the bumps.

1876 Invention of telephones

1830s Invention of computers and electric motor